AF421311

Welcome to "Dream Big, Plan Bigger" Journal!

Provided to you by Sense.

This journal is designed to help you set and achieve your most ambitious goals. Inside, you'll find tools and pages to guide you through setting goals, tracking your progress, and reflecting on your journey.

Sense.

Think of Sense as your go-to for reflecting and growing. We provide practical tools to help you turn your ambitions into achievements.

Turn the page to learn how to make the most of this journal!

How to use this journal

✏️ Use this journal whenever you have a goal, big or small.

✏️ Start by filling out the SMART goals section.

✏️ Use the lined pages for planning, note-taking, and learning.

✏️ At the end of each week, fill out the reflection page to assess your progress.

✏️ Use the doodle pages to brainstorm, plan, or unwind.

✏️ For weekly goals, utilize the weekly reflection pages.

✏️ For monthly goals, start with the monthly planner at the beginning of each month.

✏️ This journal is designed for 3 months (12 weeks, 84 days).

✏️ For shorter goals (less than 5 days), use the extra pages to detail your observations and areas for improvement.

Ready to set your first goal?

A goal without a plan is just a wish.

Month/Week Plan

Month name:

Important dates & notes:

____

____

____

____

____

____

Set your SMART goal!

1) What exactly do you want to achieve?

____

2) How will you measure progress and know when the goal is achieved?

____

3) Is this goal realistic given your resources and constraints?

4) How does this goal align with your broader objectives and values?

5) What is the deadline for achieving this goal?

Action steps

What are the specific steps you need to take to achieve this goal?

Progress tracker

Date started: __/__/____

Target completion date: __/__/____

Current status:

Notes/challenges:

Take a moment to reflect on your goal!

What were your key achievements?

What challenges did you face?

What lessons did you learn?

Were there any unexpected outcomes?

How can you improve or adapt your approach next time?

Did this goal bring you closer to your long-term vision?

Week Plan

Important dates & notes:

____

____

____

____

____

____

Set your SMART goal!

1) What exactly do you want to achieve?

____

____

2) How will you measure progress and know
when the goal is achieved?

____

____

3) Is this goal realistic given your resources and constraints?

____

4) How does this goal align with your broader objectives and values?

____

5) What is the deadline for achieving this goal?

____

Action steps

What are the specific steps you need to take to achieve this goal?

____

____

____

____

Progress tracker

Date started: __/__/____

Target completion date: __/__/____

Current status:

Notes/challenges:

Take a moment to reflect on your goal!

What were your key achievements?

What challenges did you face?

What lessons did you learn?

Were there any unexpected outcomes?

How can you improve or adapt your approach next time?

Did this goal bring you closer to your long-term vision?

Week Plan

Important dates & notes:

____

____

____

____

____

____

Set your SMART goal!

1) What exactly do you want to achieve?

____

____

2) How will you measure progress and know when the goal is achieved?

____

____

3) Is this goal realistic given your resources and constraints?

4) How does this goal align with your broader objectives and values?

5) What is the deadline for achieving this goal?

Action steps

What are the specific steps you need to take to achieve this goal?

Progress tracker

Date started: __/__/____

Target completion date: __/__/____

Current status:

Notes/challenges:

Take a moment to reflect on your goal!

What were your key achievements?

What challenges did you face?

What lessons did you learn?

Were there any unexpected outcomes?

How can you improve or adapt your approach next time?

Did this goal bring you closer to your long-term vision?

Week Plan

Important dates & notes:

____

____

____

____

____

____

Set your SMART goal!

1) What exactly do you want to achieve?

____

____

2) How will you measure progress and know when the goal is achieved?

____

____

3) Is this goal realistic given your resources and constraints?

4) How does this goal align with your broader objectives and values?

5) What is the deadline for achieving this goal?

Action steps

What are the specific steps you need to take to achieve this goal?

Progress tracker

Date started: __/__/____

Target completion date: __/__/____

Current status:

Notes/challenges:

Take a moment to reflect on your goal!

What were your key achievements?

What challenges did you face?

What lessons did you learn?

Were there any unexpected outcomes?

How can you improve or adapt your approach next time?

Did this goal bring you closer to your long-term vision?

Week Plan

Important dates & notes:

Set your SMART goal!

1) What exactly do you want to achieve?

2) How will you measure progress and know
when the goal is achieved?

3) Is this goal realistic given your resources and constraints?

4) How does this goal align with your broader objectives and values?

5) What is the deadline for achieving this goal?

Action steps

What are the specific steps you need to take to achieve this goal?

Progress tracker

Date started: __/__/____

Target completion date: __/__/____

Current status:

Notes/challenges:

Take a moment to reflect on your goal!

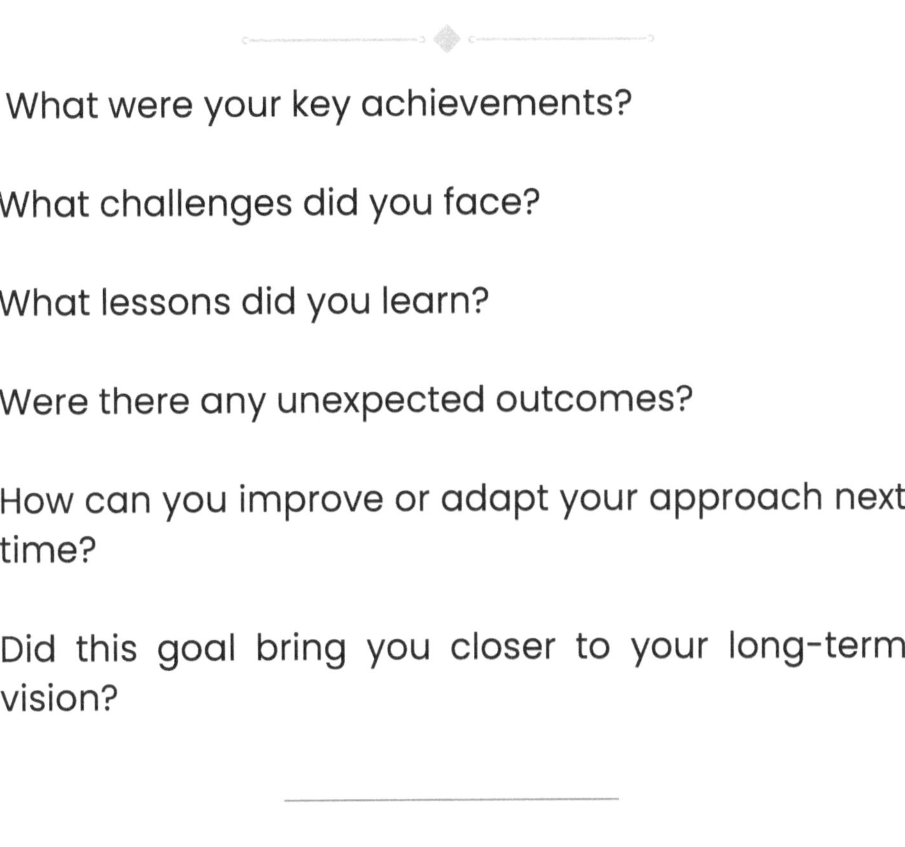

What were your key achievements?

What challenges did you face?

What lessons did you learn?

Were there any unexpected outcomes?

How can you improve or adapt your approach next time?

Did this goal bring you closer to your long-term vision?

Month/Week Plan

Month name:

Important dates & notes:

____

____

____

____

____

Set your SMART goal!

1) What exactly do you want to achieve?

____

____

2) How will you measure progress and know when the goal is achieved?

____

____

3) Is this goal realistic given your resources and constraints?

____

4) How does this goal align with your broader objectives and values?

____

5) What is the deadline for achieving this goal?

____

Action steps

What are the specific steps you need to take to achieve this goal?

____

____

____

____

Progress tracker

Date started: __/__/____

Target completion date: __/__/____

Current status:

Notes/challenges:

Week Plan

Important dates & notes:

____

____

____

____

____

Set your SMART goal!

1) What exactly do you want to achieve?

____

____

2) How will you measure progress and know when the goal is achieved?

____

____

3) Is this goal realistic given your resources and constraints?

____

4) How does this goal align with your broader objectives and values?

____

5) What is the deadline for achieving this goal?

____

Action steps

What are the specific steps you need to take to achieve this goal?

____

____

____

____

____

Progress tracker

Date started: __/__/____

Target completion date: __/__/____

Current status:

Notes/challenges:

Take a moment to reflect on your goal!

What were your key achievements?

What challenges did you face?

What lessons did you learn?

Were there any unexpected outcomes?

How can you improve or adapt your approach next time?

Did this goal bring you closer to your long-term vision?

Week Plan

Important dates & notes:

____

____

____

____

____

____

Set your SMART goal!

1) What exactly do you want to achieve?

____

____

2) How will you measure progress and know
when the goal is achieved?

____

____

3) Is this goal realistic given your resources and constraints?

____

4) How does this goal align with your broader objectives and values?

____

5) What is the deadline for achieving this goal?

____

Action steps

What are the specific steps you need to take to achieve this goal?

____

____

____

____

Progress tracker

Date started: __/__/____

Target completion date: __/__/____

Current status:

Notes/challenges:

Take a moment to reflect on your goal!

What were your key achievements?

What challenges did you face?

What lessons did you learn?

Were there any unexpected outcomes?

How can you improve or adapt your approach next time?

Did this goal bring you closer to your long-term vision?

Week Plan

Important dates & notes:

Set your SMART goal!

1) What exactly do you want to achieve?

2) How will you measure progress and know when the goal is achieved?

3) Is this goal realistic given your resources and constraints?

____

4) How does this goal align with your broader objectives and values?

____

5) What is the deadline for achieving this goal?

____

Action steps

What are the specific steps you need to take to achieve this goal?

____

____

____

____

____

Progress tracker

Date started: __/__/____

Target completion date: __/__/____

Current status:

Notes/challenges:

Take a moment to reflect on your goal!

What were your key achievements?

What challenges did you face?

What lessons did you learn?

Were there any unexpected outcomes?

How can you improve or adapt your approach next time?

Did this goal bring you closer to your long-term vision?

Week Plan

Important dates & notes:

Set your SMART goal!

1) What exactly do you want to achieve?

2) How will you measure progress and know
when the goal is achieved?

3) Is this goal realistic given your resources and constraints?

4) How does this goal align with your broader objectives and values?

5) What is the deadline for achieving this goal?

Action steps

What are the specific steps you need to take to achieve this goal?

Progress tracker

Date started: __/__/____

Target completion date: __/__/____

Current status:

Notes/challenges:

Take a moment to reflect on your goal!

What were your key achievements?

What challenges did you face?

What lessons did you learn?

Were there any unexpected outcomes?

How can you improve or adapt your approach next time?

Did this goal bring you closer to your long-term vision?

Month/Week Plan

Month name:

Important dates & notes:

____

____

____

____

____

____

Set your SMART goal!

1) What exactly do you want to achieve?

____

____

2) How will you measure progress and know when the goal is achieved?

____

____

3) Is this goal realistic given your resources and constraints?

____

4) How does this goal align with your broader objectives and values?

____

5) What is the deadline for achieving this goal?

____

Action steps

What are the specific steps you need to take to achieve this goal?

____

____

____

____

____

Progress tracker

Date started: __/__/____

Target completion date: __/__/____

Current status:

Notes/challenges:

Take a moment to reflect on your goal!

What were your key achievements?

What challenges did you face?

What lessons did you learn?

Were there any unexpected outcomes?

How can you improve or adapt your approach next time?

Did this goal bring you closer to your long-term vision?

Week Plan

Important dates & notes:

____

____

____

____

____

____

Set your SMART goal!

1) What exactly do you want to achieve?

____

____

2) How will you measure progress and know
when the goal is achieved?

____

____

3) Is this goal realistic given your resources and constraints?

____

4) How does this goal align with your broader objectives and values?

____

5) What is the deadline for achieving this goal?

____

Action steps

What are the specific steps you need to take to achieve this goal?

____

____

____

____

Progress tracker

Date started: __/__/____

Target completion date: __/__/____

Current status:

Notes/challenges:

Take a moment to reflect on your goal!

What were your key achievements?

What challenges did you face?

What lessons did you learn?

Were there any unexpected outcomes?

How can you improve or adapt your approach next time?

Did this goal bring you closer to your long-term vision?

Week Plan

Important dates & notes:

____

____

____

____

____

____

Set your SMART goal!

1) What exactly do you want to achieve?

____

____

2) How will you measure progress and know when the goal is achieved?

____

____

3) Is this goal realistic given your resources and constraints?

4) How does this goal align with your broader objectives and values?

5) What is the deadline for achieving this goal?

Action steps

What are the specific steps you need to take to achieve this goal?

Progress tracker

Date started: __/__/____

Target completion date: __/__/____

Current status:

Notes/challenges:

Take a moment to reflect on your goal!

What were your key achievements?

What challenges did you face?

What lessons did you learn?

Were there any unexpected outcomes?

How can you improve or adapt your approach next time?

Did this goal bring you closer to your long-term vision?

Week Plan

Important dates & notes:

____

____

____

____

____

____

Set your SMART goal!

1) What exactly do you want to achieve?

____

____

2) How will you measure progress and know when the goal is achieved?

____

____

3) Is this goal realistic given your resources and constraints?

____

4) How does this goal align with your broader objectives and values?

____

5) What is the deadline for achieving this goal?

____

Action steps

What are the specific steps you need to take to achieve this goal?

____

____

____

____

____

Progress tracker

Date started: __/__/____

Target completion date: __/__/____

Current status:

Notes/challenges:

Take a moment to reflect on your goal!

What were your key achievements?

What challenges did you face?

What lessons did you learn?

Were there any unexpected outcomes?

How can you improve or adapt your approach next time?

Did this goal bring you closer to your long-term vision?

Week Plan

Important dates & notes:

Set your SMART goal!

1) What exactly do you want to achieve?

2) How will you measure progress and know
when the goal is achieved?

3) Is this goal realistic given your resources and constraints?

4) How does this goal align with your broader objectives and values?

5) What is the deadline for achieving this goal?

Action steps

What are the specific steps you need to take to achieve this goal?

Progress tracker

Date started: __/__/____

Target completion date: __/__/____

Current status:

Notes/challenges:

Take a moment to reflect on your goal!

What were your key achievements?

What challenges did you face?

What lessons did you learn?

Were there any unexpected outcomes?

How can you improve or adapt your approach next time?

Did this goal bring you closer to your long-term vision?

You've reached the end of the road!

Hopefully, you've conquered at least one goal
along the way

*"Success is not in never falling, but in rising every
time we fall."*

One goal achieved is always better than none.

Use the next five pages to reflect, doodle, or
anything you want!

If you enjoyed this journal and it helped you
achieve something, consider purchasing it again
to start a new journey!

For feedback and suggestions, WhatsApp: +91
9502864503

Sense.

Our doodles